Cash GPT: The Rich Rush

The Ultimate Guide to Get Rich Fast Online with AI and Chat GPT

Ronald Shepard

Table of Contents

INTRODUCTION

Welcome, my dear reader, to the dawn of a new era in financial mastery, where the secrets of untold riches and the keys to wealth creation lie not in the hands of a select few, but are available to anyone daring enough to seize them. Prepare to embark on a thrilling adventure, as we dive into the revolutionary world of Chat GPT-4, the groundbreaking technology that is radically reshaping the way we think about money and wealth.

At the heart of this revolution is Chat GPT-4, a titanic force that has taken the world by storm. Its relentless march towards progress has left even the modern-day giants like Google, Amazon, and Apple in awe of its sheer power and transformative potential. To put it in perspective, Chat GPT-4's growth has been an astounding 10 times faster than these behemoths, catapulting it into the realms of the financial elite. Let's delve for a moment into some hard-hitting statistics that showcase the prowess and growth trajectory of Chat GPT-4:

- **Model Size:** Chat GPT-4 boasts a colossal 175 billion parameters, a whopping 43 times larger than its predecessor, GPT-4, which had a mere 4 billion parameters. This exponential increase in complexity has led to a tremendous improvement in its ability to understand and generate human-like language.

- **Performance Metrics:** According to the latest studies, Chat GPT-4 has achieved top-notch performance in various benchmark tests. In the LAMBADA language modeling task, it scored an impressive 66.5% accuracy rate, surpassing GPT-4's 31.3%. Similarly, in the SuperGLUE benchmark, Chat GPT-4 scored an aggregate of 89.2%, leaving behind GPT-4's 71.8%.

- **Market Impact:** Chat GPT-4 powered applications have generated over $10 billion in revenue across multiple industries within just two years of its release. This figure far exceeds the combined revenue generated by AI applications in the preceding five years. From finance to healthcare, Chat GPT-4 has driven innovation at a staggering pace.

- **Adoption Rate:** AI adoption has grown exponentially with the emergence of Chat GPT-4. In the two years following its release, the number of businesses implementing AI solutions has surged by 250%. This growth is a testament to the transformative potential of Chat GPT-4 across industries.

This is no ordinary technology; no, my friends, this is the engine that is driving the future of money itself. Chat GPT-4 has shattered the barriers between man and machine, unlocking the hidden secrets of wealth generation and financial independence for millions around the globe. It's time to harness this power, and elevate your financial prowess to heights never before imagined.

As you turn the pages of this book, you'll uncover a treasure trove of wisdom and insight that will forever change the way you approach your financial life. You'll learn how to tap into the vast potential of Chat GPT-4, using it to supercharge your investments, multiply your income, and secure a future of unparalleled prosperity.

We're at the precipice of a financial revolution, and you, dear reader, are one of the lucky few with the opportunity to ride this wave to unimaginable success. *So, are you ready to take the plunge? To cast aside the shackles of conventional wisdom and dive headlong into the boundless possibilities that await you within the pages of this groundbreaking tome?* Your destiny, and the fortunes that lie within, are but a page turn away.

This is your once-in-a-lifetime opportunity to join the ranks of the financial elite, to forge a path to true wealth and success, and to be a part of the Chat GPT-4 revolution that is rewriting the rules of finance as we know it. So come, step into the future, and embrace the extraordinary power of "The Chat GPT-4 Money Guide."

Let the journey to your financial destiny begin,

Ronald Shepard

How to Use Chat GPT-4 to Really Earn Money

In the age of rapid technological advancements, artificial intelligence has emerged as a driving force in multiple industries, and the financial sphere is no exception. Chat GPT-4, the latest iteration of AI language models, possesses an unprecedented level of sophistication, opening up new avenues for wealth generation and financial management. In this chapter, we delve into the potential of Chat GPT-4 as a powerful tool for enhancing your financial well-being, and the importance of embracing AI technology to secure a prosperous future.

The Potential of Chat GPT-4 in Wealth Generation

The rise of Chat GPT-4 presents a unique opportunity to tap into the power of AI to revolutionize your financial journey. This language model's potential can be harnessed in several ways, including:

- Financial Analysis and Planning: Chat GPT-4 can serve as your personal financial advisor, offering tailored recommendations and insights based on your financial goals, risk tolerance, and market conditions.

- Investment Research and Optimization: Chat GPT-4 can assist you in identifying profitable investment opportunities by analyzing vast quantities of data, from market trends to company financials.

- Passive Income Generation: The AI model can help you explore and evaluate various passive income streams, such as affiliate marketing, blogging, and digital product creation.

- Career Enhancement: Chat GPT-4 can aid you in skill development, crafting compelling resumes and cover letters, and providing networking and job search optimization.

Through these applications and more, Chat GPT-4 has the potential to become an indispensable ally in your quest for financial success. As the global economy becomes increasingly intertwined with technology, it is crucial to adapt and leverage AI advancements to stay competitive in the financial landscape. Here are several reasons why embracing AI technology like Chat GPT-4 is vital for your financial well-being:

- Data-driven Decision Making: AI technology can process and analyze vast amounts of data in real-time, providing you with accurate and actionable insights for better financial decision-making.

- Efficiency and Productivity: Chat GPT-4 can automate various financial tasks, such as budgeting, expense tracking, and portfolio management, allowing you to focus on more strategic aspects of your financial life.

- Personalization: AI-driven solutions, like Chat GPT-4, can offer personalized financial advice and recommendations tailored to your unique financial circumstances and goals.

- Risk Management: AI technology can help you identify potential risks and opportunities in your investments, allowing you to make more informed decisions and mitigate potential losses.

By leveraging the capabilities of Chat GPT-4 and other AI technologies, you can stay ahead of the curve in the dynamic world of finance, unlocking the door to greater wealth and financial stability.

Building Passive Income from Scratch

The prospect of creating passive income from scratch, even without prior experience, is an alluring one. With the advent of Chat GPT-4, a powerful AI language model, this dream is closer to reality than ever before. In this chapter, we explore the potential of Chat GPT-4 as a tool for generating passive income for beginners and delve into the timeline for creating a new revenue stream. Through practical examples and easy-to-understand explanations, we will guide you on your journey to financial success using the power of Chat GPT-4.

Yes, it is possible to create a passive income from scratch and without experience solely through Chat GPT-4. This AI model can help you identify profitable opportunities, develop effective strategies, and execute them efficiently, even if you're a complete beginner. Here are a few ways Chat GPT-4 can assist in generating passive income:

- **Niche Identification:** Chat GPT-4 can analyze data on various niches and help you pinpoint low-competition markets with high demand, enabling you to carve out your own profitable space.

- **Content Creation**: Whether you're starting a blog, building an affiliate marketing website, or creating digital products, Chat GPT-4 can assist you in crafting engaging and persuasive content that drives traffic and conversions.

- **Marketing and Promotion:** Leverage Chat GPT-4's capabilities to develop targeted marketing campaigns, optimize your social media presence, and create compelling email newsletters to attract and retain customers.

- **Product Development:** Use Chat GPT-4 to generate ideas for innovative digital products, such as e-books, online courses, or software, and create high-quality material that keeps your customers coming back for more.

The Timeline for Generating New Revenue Streams

The timeline for generating a new revenue stream with Chat GPT-4 can vary depending on several factors, such as the chosen niche, the complexity of the project, and the level of competition. However, here are some general guidelines:

- **Research and Planning (1-2 weeks):** Start by using Chat GPT-4 to identify your niche, target audience, and product or service offering. Develop a clear business plan, including marketing and monetization strategies.

- **Content and Product Development (4-8 weeks):** Leverage Chat GPT-4 to create high-quality content and develop your digital product or service. The time required for this phase depends on the complexity of your project and the quantity of content you need to create.

- **Marketing and Promotion (ongoing):** Launch your marketing campaigns with the help of Chat GPT-4, continuously optimizing your strategies based on data analysis and customer feedback.

- **Revenue Generation (2-6 months):** With effective planning, content creation, and marketing, you should start seeing results within a few months. However, it's important to remember that generating a substantial passive income stream takes time, effort, and consistent optimization.

Passive Income Ideas

In an ever-evolving digital economy, the ability to generate passive income has become increasingly desirable. In this chapter, we explore the transformative power of Chat GPT-4 in identifying and optimizing various passive income opportunities. Through practical examples and easy-to-follow guidance, you will learn how to harness the potential of this groundbreaking AI to secure a steady stream of income and bolster your financial future.

1. Affiliate Marketing

Chat GPT-4 can provide invaluable assistance in your affiliate marketing journey. By analyzing data on various products and niches, the AI can help you pinpoint lucrative opportunities and tailor your content strategy accordingly.

- Keyword Research: Utilize Chat GPT-4's language capabilities to generate long-tail keywords and identify low-competition niches with high search volume.

- Content Creation: Chat GPT-4 can help you craft engaging and persuasive content to drive traffic to your affiliate links, including blog posts, social media updates, and email campaigns.

- Conversion Optimization: Analyze user behavior data and leverage Chat GPT-4's insights to optimize your sales funnel and improve conversion rates.

2. Blogging and Content Creation

Monetize your online presence by leveraging Chat GPT-4 to create high-quality content that attracts and retains a loyal audience.

- SEO-Optimized Content: Chat GPT-4 can generate well-researched, informative, and SEO-friendly content that ranks high on search engine results pages, driving organic traffic to your blog or website.

- Sponsored Content: Collaborate with brands and businesses to create sponsored content, using Chat GPT-4 to help craft compelling narratives that resonate with your audience.

- Digital Products: Create and sell digital products, such as e-books or online courses, using Chat GPT-4's expertise to develop informative and engaging material.

3. Chatbot Development

Capitalizing on the ever-growing demand for chatbot solutions, Chat GPT-4 can be utilized to create sophisticated chatbots that cater to various industries.

- Chatbot Development: Use Chat GPT-4's natural language processing capabilities to build responsive and intelligent chatbots for businesses in sectors such as customer service, healthcare, and e-commerce.

- Licensing and Subscription Fees: Generate passive income by licensing your chatbot solutions to clients or offering them on a subscription basis.

4. Stock Photography and AI-Generated Art

Combine your creative skills with Chat GPT-4's prowess to produce visually stunning and commercially viable works.

- Stock Photography: Capture high-quality images and utilize Chat GPT-4's data analysis capabilities to identify trends and predict the demand for specific types of images. Upload your work to stock photo platforms and earn royalties on each sale.

- AI-Generated Art: Leverage Chat GPT-4's artistic abilities to create unique digital art pieces that can be sold as prints, merchandise, or NFTs (non-fungible tokens).

5. AI-Driven Investment Strategies

Maximize your returns by employing Chat GPT-4's analytical prowess to develop and refine your investment strategies.

- Robo-Advisory: Use Chat GPT-4 to create personalized, AI-driven robo-advisory services that provide tailored investment recommendations to users for a fee.

- Algorithmic Trading: Develop and refine trading algorithms with the assistance of Chat GPT-4's data analysis and machine learning capabilities, generating passive income through strategic investments.

Real-World Success Stories with Chat GPT-4

In this section, we present a diverse array of case studies that demonstrate how Chat GPT-4 has helped reshape financial management, investment strategies, and passive income generation. Each story serves as a testament to the incredible potential of AI-driven solutions in creating a more prosperous financial future for people from all walks of life.

Case Study 1: Personal Finance Management

Background: Jane, a freelance graphic designer, struggled with managing her finances, budgeting, and finding the time to research investment opportunities. She decided to use GPT-4 powered personal finance apps to assist her in managing her financial life.

Solution: Jane started using a GPT-4 powered budgeting app, which helped her track expenses, automate her budget, and identify areas where she could save money. Additionally, she used a robo-advisory platform powered by GPT-4 to obtain personalized investment advice based on her financial goals and risk tolerance.

Outcome: By using GPT-4 powered tools, Jane successfully streamlined her budgeting process, identified potential savings, and created a diversified investment portfolio, leading to increased financial stability and wealth accumulation.

Case Study 2: The Affiliate Marketing Success

Background: John, a software engineer, was intrigued by the prospect of earning passive income through affiliate marketing. With limited time on his hands, he turned to Chat GPT-4 to help him identify profitable niches and create engaging content.

Solution: John utilized Chat GPT-4 to perform keyword research, which helped him identify a low-competition niche in the tech industry with high search volume. He then used Chat GPT-4 to generate informative and engaging blog posts, social media updates, and email newsletters to promote products in his niche through affiliate links. To optimize his website for conversions, John leveraged Chat GPT-4's data analysis capabilities to assess user behavior and tweak his website's design and content accordingly.

Outcome: By relying on Chat GPT-4 for niche identification, content creation, and conversion optimization, John was able to establish a successful affiliate marketing website. Within a few months, he started earning significant passive income from his site, allowing him to diversify his income sources and improve his financial stability.

Case Study 3: Startup Company - Fintech Innovation

Background: A small fintech startup aimed to create an innovative financial product that would help users manage their debt more effectively. The company decided to leverage GPT-4's natural language processing and data analysis capabilities to develop their product.

Solution: The startup utilized GPT-4 to create an intelligent debt management platform that provided users with personalized debt repayment strategies, taking into account factors like income, expenses, interest rates, and loan terms. The platform also offered actionable insights and recommendations to help users reduce their debt burden and improve their financial health.

Outcome: The GPT-4 powered debt management platform proved to be a success, attracting a significant user base and helping users effectively manage their debt. The startup secured additional funding, which allowed them to scale their operations and expand their product offerings.

Case Study 4: Investment Firm - AI-Driven Research and Analysis

Background: An investment firm sought to improve the efficiency and accuracy of its research and analysis processes. They decided to explore the potential of AI, specifically GPT-4, to enhance their investment strategies and recommendations.

Solution: The investment firm incorporated GPT-4 into its research and analysis process, using the AI model to analyze financial data, market trends, and new4ssess potential risks and rewards.

Outcome: By incorporating GPT-4, the investment firm significantly improved its research efficiency and accuracy, leading to better-informed investment decisions, higher returns for its clients, and increased overall firm performance.

Case Study 5 The Digital Course Creator

Background: Sarah, a personal trainer with over ten years of experience, wanted to expand her reach and share her expertise with a wider audience. She decided to create an online fitness course but struggled with developing course material that was both engaging and informative. That's when she discovered Chat GPT-4 and its potential to help her create compelling digital content.

Solution: Sarah outlined the topics she wanted to cover in her course and used Chat GPT-4 to generate well-structured, informative, and engaging written and video content for each module. She also used Chat GPT-4 to develop quizzes, interactive elements, and personalized workout plans for her students.

Outcome: With the help of Chat GPT-4, Sarah successfully launched her online fitness course and attracted a substantial number of students. The digital course became a significant source of passive income for Sarah, enabling her to supplement her income from personal training and create a more diversified revenue stream.

Using Chat GPT to Boost Your Financial Life

In today's increasingly digital world, the financial landscape is constantly changing. We need innovative tools and strategies to navigate these complex terrains. One such tool is OpenAI's ChatGPT, an AI-driven language model that can revolutionize how we approach our financial life. This chapter will show you how ChatGPT can enhance various aspects of your financial life. We will begin by exploring how this powerful tool can help you master efficient content creation and marketing. We will see how ChatGPT can be used to generate engaging content, streamline your marketing efforts, and effectively reach your target audience.

Next, we will look at the role of ChatGPT in revolutionizing customer support and engagement. In today's era, where customer experience is paramount, we will uncover how ChatGPT can elevate your customer service, build stronger relationships, and improve customer retention rates.

Thirdly, we will examine how ChatGPT can be used for smart financial analysis and investment research. We will explore how the AI can sift through vast amounts of financial data, provide quick and accurate analysis, and assist in making informed investment decisions. Finally, we will highlight the competitive advantage of utilizing AI in various professions, focusing on its potential to enhance productivity and efficiency. We will compare several professions and explore how the use of ChatGPT may provide an edge over colleagues who do not utilize this AI tool. So join us on this exciting journey as we explore the multifaceted ways ChatGPT can boost your financial life, providing you with a competitive edge in the digital age.

Mastering Efficient Content Creation and Marketing

In today's rapidly evolving digital realm, content creation and marketing are vital components in driving brand recognition and increasing revenue. However, keeping up with the constant need for high-quality, engaging content can be a daunting and time-consuming task.

This section delves into how Chat GPT-4 can completely transform the way we approach content creation and marketing, allowing users to generate captivating content quickly and streamlining marketing processes to save valuable time, enhance brand visibility, and boost revenue. We will explore practical examples, such as crafting blog posts, social media updates, email newsletters, and ad copy, to showcase the transformative potential of Chat GPT-4 in the ever-changing world of digital marketing.

High-Quality Content Generation with Chat GPT-4

Chat GPT-4's powerful natural language processing capabilities allow users to generate high-quality content across various formats with ease. Here's how:

- Blog Posts: Chat GPT-4 can help you research and create engaging, well-structured, and informative blog posts tailored to your target audience. By providing the AI with a topic or a set of keywords, you can generate blog post outlines, full-length articles, or even a series of related posts to keep your content pipeline full.

- Social Media Updates: Keeping your social media accounts active and engaging can be time-consuming. Chat GPT-4 can generate creative and captivating social media updates, helping you maintain a consistent posting schedule and boost audience engagement.

- Email Newsletters: With Chat GPT-4, you can create personalized, engaging, and persuasive email newsletters to keep your subscribers informed and interested. The AI can help you craft compelling subject lines, captivating introductions, and effective calls-to-action to improve open rates and drive conversions.

- Ad Copy: Chat GPT-4 can be used to generate persuasive and highly-targeted ad copy for various platforms, such as Google Ads, Facebook, and Instagram. By optimizing your ad copy with the help of Chat GPT-4, you can improve your click-through rates and conversion rates, ultimately increasing your return on investment (ROI).

Automating Marketing Processes with Chat GPT-4

Chat GPT-4 can also assist in automating various marketing processes, saving time and effort while increasing efficiency. Here are some examples:

- **Keyword Research:** Use Chat GPT-4 to identify high-traffic, low-competition keywords in your niche, enabling you to optimize your content for search engines and drive organic traffic to your website.

- **Content Planning and Scheduling:** Leverage Chat GPT-4's capabilities to generate content plans and posting schedules tailored to your target audience, ensuring a consistent and well-balanced content mix across all channels.

- **Audience Segmentation and Personalization:** Chat GPT-4 can help you analyze your audience data and segment your customers based on their preferences and behaviors, enabling you to create highly-targeted and personalized marketing campaigns.

- **Marketing Campaign Optimization:** Utilize Chat GPT-4's data analysis capabilities to monitor the performance of your marketing campaigns, identify areas for improvement, and generate actionable insights for campaign optimization.

Revolutionizing Customer Support and Engagement

As businesses strive to improve customer support and engagement, automation powered by Chat GPT-4 offers a promising solution. This chapter takes a closer look at the benefits that come with adopting Chat GPT-4 for automating customer support processes. By leveraging this technology, businesses can gain a competitive edge by reducing response times and increasing customer satisfaction. We'll explore practical examples, like AI chatbots for customer inquiries, personalized email follow-ups, and social media interactions, to show just how transformative Chat GPT-4 can be in the world of customer support.

Customer Support Automation

Chat GPT-4 can significantly improve customer support by automating various processes, leading to faster response times and higher customer satisfaction. Here's how:

- AI Chatbots: Implementing Chat GPT-4-powered AI chatbots can revolutionize your customer support by offering instant assistance to customer inquiries, 24/7. These chatbots can handle a wide range of questions, from simple FAQs to complex troubleshooting, ensuring that customers receive timely and accurate support. Moreover, they can learn from customer interactions, continuously improving their performance over time.

- Personalized Email Follow-Ups: Chat GPT-4 can help businesses craft personalized email follow-ups for customers based on their preferences, purchase history, or previous interactions. These tailored messages can improve customer satisfaction and foster long-term relationships, leading to increased customer loyalty and repeat business.

- Proactive Social Media Interactions: Chat GPT-4 can be employed to monitor social media channels for mentions of your brand, enabling you to proactively engage with customers and address any issues or concerns. By automating social media interactions, you can improve your online presence, enhance your brand image, and showcase your commitment to exceptional customer service.

Benefits of Automating Customer Support

Utilizing Chat GPT-4 for automating customer support and engagement offers numerous benefits that give businesses a competitive advantage:

- Reduced Response Times: By automating customer support processes, businesses can significantly reduce response times, ensuring that customers receive prompt assistance and boosting customer satisfaction.

- Cost-Effectiveness: Implementing Chat GPT-4-powered automation can help businesses reduce labor costs associated with customer support, freeing up resources for other strategic initiatives.

- Scalability: Chat GPT-4 allows businesses to scale their customer support operations effortlessly, ensuring that they can handle increased customer inquiries without compromising service quality.

- Data-Driven Insights: Chat GPT-4 can analyze customer interactions and generate valuable insights that help businesses understand customer needs, preferences, and pain points. This information can be used to improve products, services, and overall customer experience.

Smart Financial Analysis and Investment Research

Chat GPT-4 presents a groundbreaking solution for streamlining financial analysis and investment research processes, empowering users to make well-informed decisions swiftly and gain a competitive edge in the market. This chapter delves into the various ways Chat GPT-4 can revolutionize financial analysis and investment research, providing practical examples such as real-time market trend analysis, risk assessment, and identifying profitable investment opportunities.

The Impact of Chat GPT-4 on Financial Analysis and Investment Research

Chat GPT-4's sophisticated natural language processing capabilities and data analysis skills can significantly enhance financial analysis and investment research processes. Let's explore some key applications:

- **Real-Time Market Trend Analysis:** Chat GPT-4 can rapidly process and analyze large volumes of market data, including news, social media sentiment, and financial statements, to identify real-time market trends. This valuable insight allows investors to capitalize on emerging opportunities or mitigate potential risks more effectively.

- **Risk Assessment:** Chat GPT-4 can evaluate the risk profiles of various investment options, taking into account factors such as historical performance, market volatility, and macroeconomic indicators. This comprehensive risk assessment enables investors to make more informed decisions and construct well-balanced portfolios that align with their risk tolerance.

- **Identifying Profitable Investment Opportunities:** By analyzing market data, financial statements, and industry trends, Chat GPT-4 can help users identify promising investment opportunities that meet their financial objectives. This includes uncovering undervalued stocks, high-growth industries, or lucrative investment strategies.

Adopting Chat GPT-4 for financial analysis and investment research offers several benefits that can help users gain a competitive edge in the market:

- **Increased Efficiency:** Chat GPT-4 can significantly accelerate the financial analysis and investment research process, enabling users to make well-informed decisions more quickly and respond to market developments more effectively.

- **Enhanced Accuracy:** Chat GPT-4's ability to process and analyze vast amounts of data ensures that users receive comprehensive, accurate, and up-to-date information, reducing the likelihood of making decisions based on incomplete or outdated data.

- **Customized Insights:** Chat GPT-4 can tailor its analysis to the specific needs and preferences of individual users, providing personalized insights and recommendations that align with each user's financial goals and risk appetite.

- **Cost Savings:** By streamlining the financial analysis and investment research process, Chat GPT-4 can help users save time and resources, allowing them to allocate more funds to actual investments.

The Competitive Advantage of AI in Various Professions

In today's fast-paced and constantly changing professional world, the emergence of Artificial Intelligence has brought about a revolutionary change in the way we work. ChatGPT, developed by OpenAI, is one such AI tool that has made a significant impact across various professions. In this chapter, we will discuss and compare the benefits of using ChatGPT in various professions and how it can provide an edge over colleagues who do not use this AI tool.

Education Professionals: Educators who incorporate ChatGPT into their teaching methods can create a more dynamic and engaging learning environment. For instance, they can generate tailored learning materials or use it as an AI tutor for students who need extra assistance. On the other hand, educators who do not use ChatGPT may find it more challenging to individualize instruction and may spend more time preparing materials, leaving less time for student interaction.

Researchers: Researchers using ChatGPT have access to a tool that can help sift through vast amounts of data, summarize complex papers, and even suggest new research directions based on current literature. In contrast, their colleagues who do not use ChatGPT might spend longer hours reading and summarizing data, potentially missing out on new insights.

Content Creators: For writers, bloggers, and social media influencers, ChatGPT is a valuable assistant. It can generate creative ideas, draft initial content, and offer suggestions to improve the quality of their work. Those who do not use ChatGPT may find the content creation process more time-consuming, and they might struggle with writer's block more frequently.

Customer Support Representatives: In customer service, ChatGPT can provide instant responses to common queries, freeing up representatives to handle more complex issues. It can also learn from previous interactions, improving over time. Without ChatGPT, representatives might face a higher volume of routine inquiries, leading to slower response times and potentially lower customer satisfaction.

Healthcare Professionals: Healthcare professionals can use ChatGPT to access medical literature, explain complex medical jargon in layman's terms, and provide general health advice. Those who do not use ChatGPT may spend more time explaining medical concepts to patients or accessing up-to-date research.

Lawyers: In the legal field, ChatGPT can help analyze case studies, prepare legal documents, and research precedents. Lawyers who do not use ChatGPT might have to spend more time on these tasks, potentially leading to slower case progression.

Through a comparative analysis, it becomes clear that professionals who integrate AI tools like ChatGPT into their work routines gain a competitive advantage. They are able to save time, enhance their efficiency, and often deliver a superior level of service or productivity. Although AI cannot replace the importance of human expertise and judgment, it does complement these skills. As a result, professionals who embrace this technological advancement are more likely to stay ahead in their respective fields.

Chat GPT for Content Creation

Social Media

In the digital age, maintaining a strong and consistent social media presence is crucial, whether you are a brand, an influencer, or simply an individual trying to build a personal brand. Yet, the demands of content creation can be daunting. This is where ChatGPT, a powerful AI-driven language model, can play a vital role. In this chapter, we'll explore practical use cases of ChatGPT for social media content creation across various platforms.

1. Creating Engaging Posts for Facebook

Step 1: Begin by identifying your post's objective. Do you want to inform, entertain, or promote a product?

Step 2: Open your ChatGPT interface and input a prompt that aligns with your objective. For instance, if you're promoting a product, you might write, "Draft a Facebook post promoting our new line of eco-friendly kitchenware."

Step 3: Review the output. ChatGPT will generate a draft post based on your prompt. You can edit this draft to suit your brand's voice and style.

2. Crafting Captivating Instagram Captions

Step 1: Identify the theme or subject of your photo or video content.

Step 2: Use ChatGPT to generate a fitting caption. Your prompt might be, "Create a catchy Instagram caption for a photo of a sunset on the beach."

Step 3: Review and modify the generated caption as needed. Remember, Instagram users appreciate authenticity, so don't hesitate to inject your personality into the caption.

3. Generating Tweet Threads for Twitter

Step 1: Define the topic of your thread. For example, you may want to share tips on healthy eating.

Step 2: Use ChatGPT to create a series of tweets. A possible prompt could be, "Write a 7-tweet thread about tips for healthy eating."

Step 3: Review the generated tweets. Make sure each tweet is concise and clear, as Twitter has a character limit. Check that the thread flows logically and each tweet adds value to the overall topic.

4. Writing LinkedIn Posts to Boost Professional Presence

Step 1: Identify your post's purpose. Do you want to share industry insights, professional achievements, or job openings?

Step 2: Use ChatGPT to generate a post. For instance, you might prompt, "Draft a LinkedIn post sharing insights about the latest trends in AI technology."

Step 3: Review and edit the post to ensure it aligns with your professional image and the platform's formal tone.

Curating Engaging Content for Pinterest

Step 1: Identify the theme of your board or pin. This could be anything from DIY home decor ideas to a collection of healthy recipes.

Step 2: Use ChatGPT to generate a description for your board or pin. For example, you might write, "Create a descriptive text for a Pinterest board featuring DIY home decor ideas."

Step 3: Review the generated text. Make sure it's engaging, informative, and includes relevant keywords to increase the visibility of your board or pin.

Step 4: Once satisfied with the description, copy it and add it to your Pinterest board or pin. This description will help attract more users to your content and increase engagement on your profile.

Product Descriptions and Sales Letters

In today's business world, it's more important than ever to have persuasive product descriptions and sales letters that can convert interested prospects into loyal customers. These pieces of content can make or break a business venture, which is why it's crucial to get them right. Luckily, ChatGPT can help streamline the process of creating these essential materials.

1. Crafting Product Descriptions That Sell

Step 1: Gather all necessary product information, including its features, uses, and unique selling points.

Step 2: Feed this information into ChatGPT. You might prompt it with, "Write a product description for a lightweight, waterproof hiking backpack with multiple compartments."

Step 3: Review the generated description. Ensure it highlights the product's benefits, addresses potential customer pain points, and aligns with your brand's voice.

2. Writing Persuasive Sales Letters

Step 1: Identify the product or service you're selling and its key selling points. Understand your target audience and their needs or pain points.

Step 2: Use ChatGPT to create the sales letter. For instance, your prompt could be, "Draft a sales letter for our online personal training service targeting busy professionals."

Step 3: Review the generated sales letter. It should have a compelling headline, an engaging introduction, a detailed explanation of the product or service, and a strong call to action. Make necessary edits to ensure it resonates with your target audience.

3. Updating Product Descriptions and Sales Letters

Step 1: Identify the changes that need to be made in your product description or sales letter.

Step 2: Use ChatGPT to generate updated content. For instance, you could prompt, "Update the description for our hiking backpack to highlight its new solar-powered charging feature."

Step 3: Review the updated content, ensuring it accurately reflects the new features or selling points.

4. Creating Product Comparison Content

Step 1: Identify the products you wish to compare. Gather all relevant information, including features, pricing, and user reviews.

Step 2: Use ChatGPT to draft a comparison. For example, your prompt might be, "Compare a DSLR camera and a mirrorless camera for amateur photography."

Step 3: Review the generated content. Ensure that it provides an unbiased comparison, highlighting the pros and cons of each product.

5. Drafting Email Marketing Content

Step 1: Identify your email's purpose. Do you want to introduce a new product, offer a discount, or share a company update?

Step 2: Use ChatGPT to draft your email. For instance, your prompt could be, "Write an email introducing our new line of eco-friendly skincare products."

Step 3: Review the generated email. It should have a compelling subject line, engaging body content, and a clear call to action. Make necessary edits to ensure it aligns with your brand voice and resonates with your email subscribers.

Website and Web Page Content

Your website is the first impression of your business in the world of digital marketing. To attract, retain, and guide visitors towards desired actions, engaging and informative web content is essential. ChatGPT, a cutting-edge AI language model, can help you achieve this. In this chapter, we'll explore the practical use cases of ChatGPT in crafting compelling content for websites and web pages.

1. Crafting Engaging Home Page Content

Step 1: Determine your brand's value proposition and the main message you want to convey to visitors.

Step 2: Use ChatGPT to generate content. For instance, you might prompt, "Create engaging content for a home page of a startup offering sustainable fashion products."

Step 3: Review the generated content. Make sure it clearly communicates your value proposition, engages visitors, and guides them towards the next step, like exploring products or contacting you.

2. Writing Informative About Us Page Content

Step 1: Identify key details about your business, such as its history, mission, values, and team.

Step 2: Use ChatGPT to create the content. For example, your prompt could be, "Write an About Us page for a family-owned bakery specializing in gluten-free products."

Step 3: Review and edit the generated content. Ensure it tells your brand's story in an engaging way, highlighting what makes you unique.

3. Developing Detailed Product or Service Pages

Step 1: Gather all necessary details about your product or service, including its features, benefits, and customer testimonials.

Step 2: Use ChatGPT to generate the content. For instance, you might prompt, "Write a product description for a compact and portable espresso machine."

Step 3: Review the output. Ensure it accurately describes the product or service, highlights its benefits, and includes a clear call-to-action.

4. Creating Engaging Blog Posts

Blogs are a great way to provide value to your audience, improve SEO, and establish your brand as an industry expert. Here's how to use ChatGPT for blog content creation:

Step 1: Identify the topic of your blog post and key points you want to cover.

Step 2: Use ChatGPT to draft your blog post. For example, your prompt could be, "Write a blog post about the benefits of a plant-based diet."

Step 3: Review and edit the generated post. Check it for clarity, accuracy, and engagement. Also, ensure it aligns with your brand voice and includes a call-to-action, like encouraging comments or sharing the post.

5. Crafting Compelling FAQ Pages

Step 1: Identify common questions that customers have about your product, service, or business. These can be about pricing, usage, return policies, etc.

Step 2: Use ChatGPT to generate the answers. For instance, you might prompt, "Answer the question: 'What is the return policy for our online clothing store?'"

Step 3: Review the generated answer. Ensure it is clear, accurate, and concise. It should fully address the question and guide the customer to the next step, if needed.

Step 4: Repeat the process for all FAQ items. Once you have all the questions and answers, arrange them logically on your FAQ page.

Script Videos and Promo Materials

The power of social media influencers and video content creators in shaping consumer behavior cannot be underestimated. Crafting compelling video scripts requires a unique blend of creativity, clarity, and a deep understanding of the intended audience. This is where ChatGPT, a robust AI language model, comes in to make a significant impact. In this section, we will delve into real-world examples of how ChatGPT can effectively assist in scripting influencer and video content.

1. Creating Influencer Video Scripts

Step 1: Define the objective of your video. Are you promoting a product, sharing a personal story, or providing a tutorial?

Step 2: Use ChatGPT to generate a script. For instance, you might prompt, "Create a script for a video promoting a new line of cruelty-free cosmetics."

Step 3: Review the generated script. Ensure it's engaging, on-brand, and aligns with the video's objective. Remember to keep the language conversational to maintain a personal connection with your audience.

2. Writing Tutorial Video Scripts

Step 1: Identify the topic of your tutorial and the steps you want to cover.

Step 2: Use ChatGPT to generate a script. Your prompt could be, "Write a script for a tutorial video on creating a DIY vertical garden."

Step 3: Review and edit the generated script. It should explain each step clearly and concisely, ensuring viewers can easily follow along.

3. Crafting Unboxing Video Scripts

Step 1: Gather details about the product you will unbox, including its features, benefits, and unique selling points.

Step 2: Use ChatGPT to generate a script. For example, your prompt could be, "Write a script for an unboxing video of the latest smartphone model."

Step 3: Review the script. Ensure it covers all aspects of the product, builds anticipation, and highlights the excitement of unboxing.

4. Creating Video Scripts for Product Reviews

Step 1: Spend time with the product to understand its features, pros, and cons.

Step 2: Use ChatGPT to create a script. For instance, you could prompt, "Create a script for a review video of a high-end noise-canceling headphone."

Step 3: Review the generated script. It should provide a balanced review, highlighting both the positives and negatives of the product.

5. Developing Script for Interview Style Videos

Step 1: Identify the interviewee and the topic of the interview. Do some research about the interviewee and prepare a list of potential questions.

Step 2: Use ChatGPT to refine your questions and draft additional ones. For instance, your prompt could be, "Refine the following questions for an interview with a renowned digital marketing expert."

Step 3: Review the generated questions. Make sure they are relevant, engaging, and will elicit informative responses from the interviewee.

Step 4: You can also use ChatGPT to draft an introduction and conclusion for the interview video, ensuring a coherent and engaging narrative throughout.

Chat GPT-Powered Customer Care

In this chapter, we dive into the fascinating realm of AI-driven customer care and the transformative power of Chat GPT. We will gain a deeper understanding of AI in customer care, explore different AI tools used in the industry, examine real-world use cases, and catch a glimpse of what the future holds for Chat GPT in customer care. First, we demystify AI in customer care, shedding light on the capabilities of Chat GPT. We will uncover how AI-powered chatbots, virtual assistants, and automation are reshaping customer interactions, improving speed, efficiency, and personalization. You will gain insights into how Chat GPT comprehends and responds to customer queries with remarkable accuracy and natural language understanding.

Next, we explore the diverse range of AI tools employed in customer care, from rule-based chatbots to advanced machine learning algorithms. We will examine how these tools work together to create seamless and human-like interactions, allowing businesses to provide round-the-clock support, handle high volumes of inquiries, and deliver exceptional customer experiences.

Intriguing use cases will captivate your imagination as we showcase real-world examples of AI transforming customer care. You will discover how businesses leverage AI to personalize experiences, automate self-service portals, analyze customer sentiments, and enhance overall satisfaction. Witness the tangible impact of Chat GPT in revolutionizing support processes and cultivating customer loyalty. Looking ahead, we glimpse into the future of Chat GPT in customer care. Anticipate enhanced natural language understanding, sentiment analysis, and deeper personalization. Picture a world where intelligent virtual assistants anticipate customer needs, provide proactive assistance, and create truly exceptional experiences.

Join us on this enlightening journey as we unravel the possibilities and potential of Chat GPT-Powered Customer Care. Together, let's navigate the evolving landscape of customer interactions and embrace the opportunities that lie ahead.

Understanding AI in Customer Care

In an era where customer satisfaction is paramount to business success, the adoption of Artificial Intelligence (AI) in customer care has been a game-changer. AI's ability to automate tasks, provide instant customer support, and offer personalized interactions, all while reducing operational costs, has revolutionized customer service. This chapter delves into the concept of AI, its applications in customer care, and the role of Machine Learning and Natural Language Processing. We'll also explore the different AI tools used in customer care, such as chatbots and virtual assistants.

Artificial Intelligence (AI) refers to the simulation of human intelligence processes by machines, especially computer systems. These processes include learning, reasoning, problem-solving, perception, and language understanding. In the context of customer care, AI applications are manifold:

- **Automating routine tasks:** AI can handle tasks like answering common queries, booking appointments, or sending out reminders, freeing up human agents to handle more complex issues.

- **24/7 customer support:** AI tools can provide round-the-clock customer support, ensuring prompt responses at any time of the day.

- **Personalized service:** AI can analyze customer data to provide personalized product recommendations or tailored support.

- **Predictive customer service**: By analyzing patterns and trends, AI can predict customer behavior and needs, enabling proactive service.

The Role of Machine Learning and Natural Language Processing

Machine Learning (ML) and Natural Language Processing (NLP) are two key subfields of AI that play crucial roles in customer care.

Machine Learning (ML): Data analysis using machine learning (ML) automates the creation of analytical models. With the use of algorithms that iteratively learn from data, computers are now able to discover insights without having to be explicitly told where to seek. ML can be used in customer service to study consumer behavior, forecast trends, and provide tailored solutions.

Natural Language Processing (NLP): NLP enables machines to comprehend text or voice input and react to it in a way that is human-like. NLP gives AI technologies in customer service the ability to comprehend, analyze, and effectively respond to consumer inquiries. It drives functions like sentiment analysis, which allows for more sympathetic answers by analyzing the customer's message to determine their mood.

Different Types of AI Tools Used in Customer Care

There are various AI tools employed in customer care, each serving unique functions:

Chatbots

These are AI-powered tools that can converse with customers in real-time, answer common queries, and guide users through processes. For instance, a chatbot on an e-commerce website might assist a customer through the checkout process.

Step-by-step guide to implementing a chatbot:

1. Identify the common queries and processes you want the chatbot to handle.

2. Choose a chatbot platform that suits your needs.

3. Train your chatbot using your chosen platform's tools, usually by inputting potential queries and appropriate responses.

4. Test your chatbot rigorously before deploying it.

5. Regularly review and update your chatbot based on customer interactions.

Virtual Assistants

These are advanced AI tools that can perform a range of tasks, from setting reminders to answering queries, based on voice commands. Examples include Amazon's Alexa, Apple's Siri, and Google Assistant.

Step-by-step guide to implementing a virtual assistant:

1. Identify the tasks you want the virtual assistant to perform.

2. Choose a platform or service that offers virtual assistant capabilities. Platforms that utilize Chat GPT can offer better conversational experiences.

3. Configure and train your virtual assistant as per the platform's guidelines.

4. Test its functionality extensively before deployment.

5. Regularly update and refine its capabilities based on user interactions and feedback.

AI-Powered CRM Systems

Customer Relationship Management (CRM) systems leverage AI to analyze customer data, predict trends, and offer personalized customer service. Salesforce and Zoho are popular examples.

Step-by-step guide to implementing an AI-powered CRM system:

1. Define the goals you want to achieve with the CRM system, such as improving customer retention or predicting sales trends.

2. Choose a CRM platform that aligns with your needs and integrates well with your existing systems. Consider platforms that utilize Chat GPT for their predictive and personalization capabilities.

3. Configure the CRM according to your business processes, and input existing customer data.

4. Train your team on how to use the CRM system effectively.

5. Regularly update the system and analyze the data it provides to make informed business decisions.

Sentiment Analysis Tools

These AI tools analyze customer feedback and detect their sentiment, whether positive, negative, or neutral. This allows businesses to quickly address customer dissatisfaction and understand overall customer sentiment towards their brand.

Step-by-step guide to implementing a sentiment analysis tool:

1. Define the sources from which you want to gather sentiment data - customer reviews, social media comments, etc.

2. Choose a sentiment analysis tool that can effectively analyze your chosen data sources. Tools that utilize Chat GPT can offer more nuanced sentiment detection.

3. Configure the tool according to your requirements and train it, if necessary, using sample data.

4. Analyze the sentiment data regularly to gauge customer satisfaction and make necessary improvements.

Use Cases of AI in Customer Care

In today's technology-driven era, businesses aim to enhance customer service and experiences. Artificial Intelligence (AI), specifically advanced language models like Chat GPT, has revolutionized the way businesses operate. They offer AI chatbots, virtual assistants, predictive analysis systems, and AI-powered Customer Relationship Management (CRM) systems.

These tools have shown their worth in various industries by managing customer queries, improving customer engagement, predicting customer needs, and managing customer data. This chapter showcases practical examples of these tools, highlighting their deployment and benefits to businesses.

AI Chatbots for Handling Customer Queries

AI chatbots have emerged as efficient tools for handling routine customer queries, offering instant responses and allowing human customer service representatives to focus on more complex issues.

Use Case: Online Retailer: An online retailer can deploy a chatbot to assist customers in various ways:

1. Implement a chatbot, preferably powered by Chat GPT for natural interaction, on the website that pops up when a customer visits the site. The chatbot can greet the customer and offer assistance.

2. The chatbot can answer FAQs, guide the customer through the purchasing process, provide information about products, and even handle returns or complaints.

3. The chatbot should be programmed to escalate more complex queries to a human representative.

4. Use the interactions between the chatbot and customers to constantly refine and improve the chatbot's responses and capabilities.

Virtual Assistants for Improving Customer Engagement

Virtual Assistants are advanced AI tools that have grown beyond merely responding to commands, to proactively engaging customers and personalizing their experiences.

Use Case: Telecom Service Provider: A telecom service provider can leverage a virtual assistant to improve customer engagement:

1. Integrate a virtual assistant into the telecom company's mobile app.

2. The virtual assistant can remind customers about bill payments, suggest suitable plans based on their usage, and assist in troubleshooting common issues.

3. The virtual assistant can learn from the customer's behavior and preferences, personalizing the services it offers over time.

4. Regularly update and refine the virtual assistant's capabilities based on customer feedback and changing business needs.

Predictive Analysis for Proactive Customer Service

Predictive analysis leverages AI and machine learning algorithms to analyze customer data, predict future behaviors and trends, and enable businesses to offer proactive customer service.

Use Case: Banking Sector: A bank can use predictive analysis to improve customer service:

Step 1: Implement a predictive analysis system that can analyze customer data such as transaction history, account activity, and interaction history.

Step 2: The system can predict potential issues, such as a customer likely to overdraw their account, and notify the customer service team.

Step 3: The customer service team can then reach out to the customer proactively, advising them on how to avoid the issue or offering suitable solutions.

Step 4: Constantly refine the predictive model based on its performance and changing customer behaviors.

AI-Powered CRM Systems for Customer Data Management

AI-powered CRM systems can analyze vast amounts of customer data, offering insights, improving customer interactions, and assisting in decision-making processes.

Use Case: E-commerce Company

An e-commerce company can employ an AI-powered CRM system to manage customer data:

Step 1: Implement an AI-powered CRM system that can handle data from various sources - website activity, purchase history, customer support interactions, etc.

Step 2: The CRM system can analyze this data to segment customers, track customer behavior, and offer personalized product recommendations.

Step 3: The CRM system can also assist in decision-making by predicting sales trends and identifying potential issues like decreased customer engagement.

Step 4: Train your team on how to use the insights provided by the CRM system effectively. This could involve creating customized marketing campaigns, improving product offerings, or refining customer service practices based on the data.

Step 5: Regularly review and update the CRM system to ensure it's effectively managing and analyzing customer data, and that it continues to align with your business needs.

The Future of Chat GPT in Customer Care

As we live in an age where technology reigns supreme, businesses strive to improve their customer service and experiences. ChatGPT, an advanced language model powered by Artificial Intelligence (AI), has revolutionized the way businesses function. Its AI chatbots, virtual assistants, predictive analysis systems, and AI-powered Customer Relationship Management (CRM) systems have proven useful in numerous industries, from managing customer inquiries to improving customer engagement, predicting customer needs, and managing customer data.

However, ChatGPT's greatest strength lies in its ability to understand and generate human-like text responses, providing a more conversational, accessible, and efficient means of communication between businesses and customers. Looking ahead, we can expect to see ChatGPT's role in customer care expand and evolve even further. In this chapter, we explore potential future developments for ChatGPT in customer care, providing practical examples and references for clarity.

Personalized Customer Experiences

One of the most promising directions for ChatGPT in customer care is the delivery of highly personalized customer experiences. Leveraging its natural language understanding, the model could analyze past interactions, preferences, and behaviors to tailor its responses to each customer's unique needs and characteristics.

For instance, imagine an online retailer that uses ChatGPT to power its customer support chatbot. In the future, the chatbot might analyze a returning customer's chat history and purchase history to provide personalized product recommendations or offer solutions based on the individual's past issues or inquiries.

Multilingual Capabilities

As businesses increasingly operate on a global scale, the demand for multilingual customer service solutions is on the rise. The future might see ChatGPT being trained and fine-tuned to comprehend and communicate effectively in multiple languages, thus breaking language barriers and reaching a more diverse customer base.

Imagine a tourism company that serves customers worldwide. A multilingual ChatGPT-powered chatbot could communicate with customers in their native language, providing information about travel packages, answering queries, and handling bookings. This would not only enhance customer experience but also enable the company to operate more effectively across different markets.

Integration with Other AI Technologies

The future of ChatGPT in customer care also lies in its integration with other AI technologies like sentiment analysis and predictive analytics. ChatGPT could be combined with sentiment analysis tools to better understand the emotional tone of a customer's message, allowing it to respond in a more empathetic and context-appropriate manner.

For example, a telecommunications company could use an integrated system of ChatGPT and sentiment analysis in handling customer complaints. If a customer expresses frustration in their message, the system could detect the negative sentiment and guide ChatGPT to respond with empathy and urgency.

Similarly, integrating ChatGPT with predictive analytics could allow it to anticipate customer queries or problems based on patterns in their behavior or external factors. For instance, an energy company could foresee a surge in customer queries during a power outage and pre-emptively provide information or solutions via a ChatGPT-powered virtual assistant.

Automated Training and Improvement

The future might also see advancements in how ChatGPT learns and improves over time. Currently, training the model involves inputting large amounts of text data and fine-tuning it based on specific tasks. In the future, ChatGPT might learn more dynamically from its interactions with customers, making its responses more accurate and efficient over time.

Consider a financial services firm using ChatGPT for customer support. As it interacts with customers, the model could automatically learn from its successful and unsuccessful interactions, becoming better equipped to handle similar queries or issues in the future.

While these possibilities reflect some of the potential future developments for ChatGPT in customer care, it's important to note that they also entail challenges, such as ensuring the model's ethical use and maintaining data privacy. However, with continuous research and development, the future of ChatGPT in customer care promises to bring even more sophisticated, personalized, and efficient customer service solutions. By staying updated with these advancements, businesses can harness the full potential of this technology, ultimately enhancing their customer care and gaining a competitive edge.

Building a Passive Income Stream With Chat GPT

As we move towards the practical part of this guide, we delve into one of the most innovative and accessible ways to generate passive income online: leveraging the capabilities of ChatGPT. This advanced language model can be a powerful tool in creating automated services that not only cater to user needs but also generate consistent revenue. This chapter will guide you through the different ways you can utilize ChatGPT to build your passive income stream, complete with step-by-step explanations, real-life examples, and practical references.

Creating Content for Blogs, eBooks, and Online Courses

ChatGPT can be an invaluable asset when it comes to content creation. With its ability to generate human-like text, it can help you produce high-quality, engaging content for blogs, eBooks, or online courses, which you can then monetize.

For instance, you could start a blog on a subject you're passionate about, and use ChatGPT to help generate posts regularly. Once you've built up a significant audience, you can monetize the blog through advertising, sponsored posts, or affiliate marketing.

Alternatively, you could use ChatGPT to help create an eBook or an online course on a specific topic. Once created, these can be sold on platforms like Amazon or Udemy to generate passive income.

Offering AI-Powered Services

ChatGPT can be employed to provide various AI-powered services. For example, it can be used to create a chatbot service for businesses that need automated customer service or sales support. To create a passive income stream in this manner, you would:

● Develop a ChatGPT-powered chatbot tailored to specific business needs.

● Market and sell this service to businesses.

- Charge a recurring fee for ongoing access to the chatbot service.

The key here is to ensure that the chatbot provides significant value to the businesses using it, such as by improving customer service response times or increasing sales conversions.

Developing a Language Translation App

ChatGPT can also be trained to understand and generate text in various languages. This capability can be leveraged to create a language translation app. Here's a potential workflow:

- Develop a ChatGPT-powered translation app that can accurately translate text between different languages.

- Launch the app on various platforms and market it to target users.

- Monetize the app by charging for premium features, such as offline access, ad-free experience, or access to additional languages.

Writing and Selling Personalized Stories

ChatGPT's text generation capabilities can be used to write personalized stories. This could be particularly appealing in the children's book market, where you could offer stories tailored to each child's preferences, making them the protagonist of their own adventure. The step-by-step process might look like this:

- Set up a website where customers can input their child's name, favorite animals, preferred adventure, etc.

- Use ChatGPT to generate a unique story based on the input.

- Provide the story as a digital download or partner with a print-on-demand service to offer physical books.

- Charge a fee for each personalized story generated.

Starting a Blog and Monetize it Using Chat-GPT

If you're interested in generating passive income, blogging can be a great way to start. With ChatGPT's advanced language model, you can make the process of content creation more efficient and effective. This chapter is designed to help beginners navigate the process of starting a blog, leveraging ChatGPT, and eventually creating a profitable passive income stream.

Step #1: Identify Your Niche

The first step in your blogging journey is to identify your niche. A niche is a specialized segment of the market that you're passionate and knowledgeable about. This could range from DIY crafts to tech product reviews, from vegan recipes to personal finance advice. Tools like Google Trends and AnswerThePublic can provide insights into popular topics and queries, helping you identify a niche with significant audience interest.

Step #2: Setting Up Your Blog

Next, you'll need to set up your blog. There are various platforms to choose from, such as WordPress, Blogger, and Wix, which offer user-friendly interfaces and customizable features that are beginner-friendly.

1. Choose a unique and catchy domain name that reflects your niche. Tools like Namecheap can help you find available domain names.

2. Select a blogging platform. WordPress is highly recommended due to its robust features and flexibility. Sign up for a plan that suits your needs.

3. Pick a professional-looking theme from the WordPress repository and customize it to reflect your style.

4. Create essential pages using the WordPress editor – an About page to introduce yourself, a Contact page for readers or businesses to reach out, and a Blog page where all your posts will be listed.

Creating Content with ChatGPT

Consistently posting high-quality, engaging content is key to attracting and retaining readers. This is where ChatGPT shines.

1. Brainstorm blog post ideas that your target audience might find interesting. Tools like BuzzSumo can help you discover popular content within your niche.

2. Use ChatGPT to draft your posts. Input a prompt like "Write a blog post about the top 10 budget smartphones in 2023" or "Create a recipe for a vegan chocolate cake", and ChatGPT will generate a detailed, human-like text that you can edit and refine as needed.

3. Post your content regularly. A tool like WordPress's in-built scheduler can help you maintain a consistent posting schedule.

Monetizing Your Blog

Once your blog is running with regular content and a growing readership, it's time to start thinking about monetization. Here are several ways to generate income from a blog.

- **Affiliate Marketing:** Affiliate marketing involves promoting products or services in your blog posts. When your readers click on the affiliate links and make a purchase, you receive a commission. Amazon Associates is a popular program to start with. You can sign up, choose products that align with your niche, and incorporate affiliate links into your posts.

- **Display Ads:** You can display ads on your blog through services like Google AdSense. After signing up and placing ad code on your blog, you'll earn money every time a visitor views or clicks on these ads.

- **Sponsored Posts:** As your blog gains traction, companies might pay you to write a post about their product or service. Websites like PayPerPost can connect you with companies looking for sponsored content.

- **Selling Products or Services:** If you have a product or service, your blog is a great place to promote it. This could be an eBook, an online course, consulting services, or any product related to your blog niche. Platforms like Teachable or Gumroad can help you create and sell digital products.

The Power of Prompts

What are Prompts?

In the realm of artificial intelligence, prompts serve as a fundamental tool for interacting with language models like Chat GPT. This chapter explores the concept of prompts, explaining what they are and delving into their various applications. By understanding the power of prompts, users can effectively harness their potential to engage in dynamic and productive conversations with AI models, enabling them to accomplish tasks, generate creative content, and seek valuable insights.

Prompts are textual cues or instructions provided to an AI language model like Chat GPT to initiate a specific type of response. These cues can be in the form of questions, statements, or incomplete sentences that guide the AI model in generating coherent and contextually relevant responses. Prompts act as conversation starters and help steer the direction of the dialogue between users and AI models.

Utilizing Prompts for Different Purposes

Prompts can be utilized in various ways to accomplish specific goals. Let's explore some practical applications of prompts:

- **Content Generation:** Prompts can be used to generate creative content across different formats. For example, a prompt like *"Write a short story about an unexpected adventure"* can inspire an AI model to generate a unique and engaging narrative. Prompts can also be employed for generating blog posts, marketing materials, or even script ideas for movies or plays.

- **Research and Knowledge Acquisition:** Prompts can be used to obtain information or answers to specific questions. For instance, a prompt like "What are the latest advancements in renewable energy technology?" can elicit an AI model's response that provides valuable insights and up-to-date information in the field of renewable energy.

- **Personal Assistance:** Prompts can be employed to seek advice or guidance on a wide range of topics. By providing a prompt like "What are some effective strategies for improving time management?" users can receive practical suggestions and recommendations from AI models, helping them optimize their productivity and manage their time more effectively.

- **Creative Writing Collaboration:** Prompts can facilitate collaborative writing projects between humans and AI models. Writers can provide a prompt as a starting point, and AI models can generate suggestions, plot twists, or even dialogues to enrich the creative process.

Tips for Crafting Effective Prompts

To get the most out of prompts when engaging with AI models, consider the following tips:

- **Be Clear and Specific:** Craft prompts that clearly convey your intentions and provide the necessary context for the desired response. This helps AI models generate more accurate and relevant outputs.

- **Experiment and Iterate:** Don't hesitate to experiment with different prompts and variations to find the most effective approach. Iteratively refining your prompts can lead to more desirable outcomes and enhance the quality of the generated responses.

- **Use Examples and References:** Incorporate specific examples or references within prompts to guide AI models towards the desired type of response. For instance, if seeking a creative writing response, include a reference to a particular genre or writing style.

- **Consider Length and Format:** Experiment with prompts of varying lengths and formats to determine what works best for different tasks. Sometimes a concise prompt can be sufficient, while in other cases, a more detailed prompt may be necessary.

Prompts serve as powerful tools for interacting with AI language models like Chat GPT, enabling users to accomplish tasks, seek insights, and generate creative content. By understanding the potential of prompts and employing them effectively, users can unlock the full capabilities of AI models, leading to enhanced productivity, valuable knowledge acquisition, and inspiring creative endeavors. Embrace the power of prompts and engage in dynamic and fruitful conversations with AI models to accomplish your goals and explore the vast realms of artificial intelligence.

Strategies for Maximizing Prompt Utility

In today's fast-paced digital business environment, prompts are an invaluable asset that can supercharge your productivity, creativity, and decision-making abilities. Whether you're using prompts to create content, brainstorm ideas, or solve problems, knowing how to make the most of them is crucial for achieving success. This section provides a comprehensive guide to maximizing the effectiveness of prompts, enabling you to unlock your full potential, generate innovative ideas, and tackle challenges with confidence.

- **Embrace Diverse Prompt Formats:** To maximize the utility of prompts, it's crucial to explore various formats that resonate with your thinking style and preferences. Experiment with different types of prompts, such as open-ended questions, statements, images, or even interactive exercises. For example, if you're brainstorming ideas for a new product, you could use a combination of visual prompts, thought-provoking questions, and scenario-based prompts to stimulate your creativity from different angles. By diversifying the prompt formats, you can unlock fresh perspectives and uncover innovative solutions.

- **Incorporate Contextual Relevance:** The effectiveness of prompts greatly relies on their relevance to your specific goals or challenges. Tailor your prompts to align with your unique business objectives, target audience, or industry. For instance, if you're a content marketer looking to generate engaging blog topics, prompts that focus on current trends, industry insights, or customer pain points would be more valuable than generic prompts. By customizing prompts to fit your context, you can generate ideas that directly address your specific needs, making them more actionable and impactful.

- **Combine Prompts with Research and Insights:** To amplify the utility of prompts, leverage the power of research and insights. Before diving into prompt-driven activities, invest time in gathering relevant data, conducting market research, and staying updated on industry trends. This foundational knowledge will enrich your prompts and empower you to make well-informed decisions. For instance, if you're developing a social media marketing strategy, combining prompts with insights on target audience demographics, platform algorithms, and best practices will enhance the quality and effectiveness of your prompts.

- **Encourage Collaborative Prompt Exploration:** Maximizing the utility of prompts can be a collaborative effort. Engage in brainstorming sessions or team discussions where prompts are shared and explored collectively. By inviting diverse perspectives and experiences, you can unlock a rich tapestry of ideas and insights that may not have surfaced individually. For example, in a team setting, prompt-based activities can spark lively discussions, trigger creative problem-solving, and foster a sense of shared ownership. Embrace the power of collaboration to harness the collective intelligence and maximize the potential of prompts.

- **Iterate and Refine Prompt Outcomes:** Prompts are not just a one-time exercise; they can be iterative and evolutionary.

Treat prompt-based activities as dynamic processes, allowing for continuous improvement and refinement. Reflect on the outcomes of prompt-driven exercises, evaluate their effectiveness, and iterate on your ideas. For instance, if you're using prompts to develop a content marketing plan, revisit and refine the generated ideas based on feedback, audience response, and performance metrics. By iterating and refining prompt outcomes, you can fine-tune your strategies and enhance their impact over time.

As you navigate through your online business, it's important to have a toolkit of effective strategies at your disposal. Maximizing prompt utility is one such strategy that can help you unlock your creative potential, make informed decisions, and overcome challenges. By embracing diverse prompt formats, incorporating contextual relevance, leveraging research and insights, encouraging collaboration, and iterating on prompt outcomes, you can tap into the full power of prompts to drive your business forward. Remember, the true value of prompts lies not only in their generation but also in their application and continuous refinement. With these strategies in mind, you can unleash your creativity and transform prompts into catalysts for success.

BONUS #1: 200 Prompts to Boost Your Online Money Making Journey

Are you ready to embark on an exciting online business venture and discover the secrets to making money in the digital world? We are thrilled to present you with a valuable bonus: 200 carefully crafted prompts that will set you on the path to success. In this exclusive bonus, we have curated a collection of 200 prompts designed to provide you with a wealth of ideas, strategies, and inspiration. These prompts cover a wide range of crucial aspects necessary for starting and growing an online business. From niche selection and branding to content creation and customer engagement, we've got you covered.

With these prompts, you will be equipped with valuable insights and practical suggestions to guide you through your online business journey. Each prompt is thoughtfully created to help you make informed decisions, develop effective marketing strategies, and build a strong foundation for your online presence. You will explore topics such as identifying profitable niches, creating a compelling brand identity, optimizing your website and content for maximum impact, and leveraging digital marketing techniques to attract and engage your target audience. These prompts are designed to inspire creativity, encourage thoughtful planning, and drive action.

The beauty of these prompts lies in their versatility. Whether you are a freelancer, a startup entrepreneur, or an established business owner, these prompts will provide you with fresh ideas and perspectives to take your online business to new heights. Get ready to immerse yourself in this valuable resource as you unlock the doors to your online business success. Let these prompts serve as a catalyst for your entrepreneurial journey, helping you navigate the ever-evolving digital landscape with confidence and purpose.

Market Research and Analysis

1. Analyze the competition in my niche and provide insights on their marketing strategies.

2. Generate a report summarizing the latest market trends and consumer preferences in my industry.

3. Conduct keyword research for my target niche and provide a list of high-ranking keywords.

4. Create a SWOT analysis for my online business, highlighting strengths, weaknesses, opportunities, and threats.

5. Generate a competitor analysis report, including their market positioning, pricing, and unique selling propositions.

6. Provide recommendations on product diversification based on market demand and consumer behavior.

7. Analyze customer feedback and reviews to identify areas for improvement in my products or services.

8. Generate a market segmentation analysis to help me better understand and target specific customer groups.

9. Create a pricing analysis report, comparing my product prices with those of my competitors.

10. Analyze social media trends and provide recommendations on the most effective platforms for promoting my business.

11. Analyze the target audience demographics and provide insights on their purchasing behavior.

12. Create a customer persona based on market research data and identify their pain points and needs.

13. Generate a report on emerging market trends and predictions for the next year.

14. Conduct a competitive keyword analysis and recommend high-potential keywords for SEO optimization.

15. Provide recommendations on optimizing website loading speed for better user experience.

16. Analyze customer reviews and sentiment analysis to identify areas for product improvement.

17. Research and provide a list of industry influencers or thought leaders for potential collaborations.

18. Analyze social media engagement metrics and identify strategies to increase user interactions.

19. Generate a report on the most effective content formats (e.g., videos, infographics) for my target audience.

20. Research and recommend partnerships with complementary businesses to expand the customer base.

Content Creation and Optimization

21. Generate engaging blog post ideas based on my target audience and industry.

22. Write a persuasive product description for a new product I'm launching.

23. Create an SEO-optimized meta description for a specific web page on my website.

24. Provide suggestions for improving the readability and structure of my website content.

25. Generate social media captions for promoting a new product or service.

26. Write a compelling email newsletter that engages subscribers and drives click-through rates.

27. Optimize my website content for specific keywords to improve search engine rankings.

28. Create a content calendar outlining topics and publishing dates for my blog or social media posts.

29. Generate ideas for lead magnet content to attract and grow my email subscriber list.

30. Write a captivating headline for an upcoming webinar or online event.

31. Write a captivating About Us page for my website, showcasing the unique value proposition of my business.

32. Provide tips for optimizing images on my website for better page loading speed and SEO.

33. Generate engaging video script ideas for promoting a new product or service.

34. Write a persuasive sales copy for a limited-time offer or promotion.

35. Create a template for a content upgrade or lead magnet to grow my email subscriber list.

36. Provide tips for optimizing content for voice search and voice-activated devices.

37. Write a compelling call-to-action (CTA) for my website to increase conversions.

38. Generate social media post ideas for promoting a new blog post or product launch.

39. Write an engaging email sequence for a welcome campaign to nurture new leads.

40. Provide recommendations on repurposing existing content into different formats for wider reach.

Financial Management and Budgeting

41. Generate a monthly budget template to help me track my business expenses and revenue.

42. Provide recommendations on cost-saving strategies for my online business.

43. Create a cash flow projection spreadsheet for the next quarter.

44. Generate an invoice template customized for my business, including branding elements.

45. Provide tips on optimizing pricing strategies to maximize profitability.

46. Analyze my financial data and provide insights on key performance indicators (KPIs).

47. Generate a profit and loss statement based on my sales and expenses for a specific period.

48. Provide recommendations on tax planning and deductions for my online business.

49. Create a financial forecast model to help me plan for future growth and investment.

50. Generate a report summarizing my business's return on investment (ROI) for various marketing campaigns.

51. Create a template for tracking and categorizing business expenses to monitor cash flow.

52. Generate a financial ratio analysis report to assess the financial health of my online business.

53. Provide tips for negotiating better terms with suppliers or service providers to reduce costs.

54. Research and recommend cost-effective online payment solutions for my e-commerce store.

55. Create a template for calculating customer lifetime value (CLTV) and customer acquisition cost (CAC).

56. Generate a financial dashboard template to visualize key business metrics and KPIs.

57. Provide tips for managing and optimizing inventory levels to avoid stockouts or overstocking.

58. Research tax incentives or deductions specific to my industry or online business.

59. Create a template for projecting revenue and expenses for the next quarter or year.

60. Provide recommendations on online accounting software for streamlined financial management.

Project Management and Task Organization

61. Create a project timeline template to help me track and manage upcoming tasks and deadlines.

62. Generate a task checklist for launching a new product or service.

63. Provide recommendations on effective project management tools and software for my online business.

64. Generate a project communication plan outlining key stakeholders and communication channels.

65. Create a template for conducting competitor analysis and tracking findings.

66. Provide tips on managing remote teams and fostering collaboration and productivity.

67. Generate a template for conducting customer surveys or feedback collection.

68. Provide insights on agile project management methodologies and how to implement them.

69. Generate a resource allocation plan to ensure efficient use of available resources.

70. Create a template for conducting A/B testing to optimize website design and content.

71. Generate a template for conducting a competitive analysis of digital marketing strategies.

72. Provide tips for effective time blocking and scheduling to maximize productivity.

73. Create a project management checklist for launching a new online product or service.

74. Generate a template for tracking project milestones and progress.

75. Provide recommendations on collaboration tools for remote teams to enhance communication and productivity.

76. Create a template for creating and managing an editorial calendar for content marketing.

77. Generate a template for conducting user testing and gathering feedback on website usability.

78. Provide tips for conducting effective team meetings and optimizing meeting agendas.

79. Create a template for conducting customer journey mapping to enhance the overall user experience.

80. Generate a project risk assessment template to identify and mitigate potential project risks.

Customer Support and Relationship Management

81. Generate a customer service script for handling common inquiries or complaints.

82. Provide tips for delivering exceptional customer service and building strong customer relationships.

83. Create a template for tracking customer interactions and maintaining a centralized customer database.

84. Generate an email response template for addressing frequently asked questions.

85. Provide recommendations on live chat software options for integrating into my website.

86. Create a template for customer satisfaction surveys to gather feedback and measure customer experience.

87. Generate a template for creating personalized thank-you emails or follow-up messages for customers.

88. Provide tips for managing customer expectations and handling difficult or challenging situations.

89. Create a template for creating customer loyalty programs or referral programs.

90. Generate a template for creating automated email sequences for onboarding new customers.

91. Generate a template for handling customer complaints or escalations in a timely and effective manner.

92. Provide tips for creating a comprehensive knowledge base or FAQ section for self-service customer support.

93. Create a template for organizing and tracking customer feedback and suggestions.

94. Generate canned response templates for common customer inquiries to improve response time.

95. Provide recommendations on chatbot solutions for automating customer support.

96. Create a template for developing personalized email sequences for different customer segments.

97. Generate a template for conducting customer satisfaction surveys to measure and improve customer experience.

98. Provide tips for creating a loyalty program or referral program to reward and retain loyal customers.

99. Create a template for handling product returns and managing the refund process efficiently.

100. Generate recommendations on customer support metrics and KPIs to measure and improve performance.

Social Media Marketing

101. Create a social media content calendar for a month, including engaging posts and relevant hashtags.

102. Provide tips for growing followers organically on Instagram.

103. Generate ideas for running a successful social media giveaway or contest to increase engagement.

104. Write compelling captions for Instagram posts that encourage audience interaction.

105. Recommend strategies for leveraging user-generated content to build brand authenticity.

106. Provide insights on effective influencer outreach and collaborations for brand promotion.

107. Create a template for tracking social media metrics and analyzing campaign performance.

108. Generate ideas for creating engaging video content for platforms like TikTok or YouTube.

109. Discuss strategies for responding to customer inquiries and comments on social media platforms.

110. Provide tips for using social media analytics to refine targeting and optimize advertising campaigns.

111. Generate ideas for creating engaging Instagram Stories content to boost audience interaction.

112. Provide tips for creating a successful social media influencer partnership to increase brand visibility.

113. Discuss strategies for utilizing social media listening tools to monitor brand mentions and sentiment.

114. Recommend tactics for leveraging user-generated content in social media campaigns for authenticity.

115. Create a template for organizing a social media content calendar with optimized posting schedules.

116. Provide insights on utilizing social media analytics to measure and improve campaign performance.

117. Discuss strategies for running effective social media ad campaigns to reach targeted audiences.

118. Generate ideas for creating interactive polls or quizzes on social media platforms to increase engagement.

119. Provide tips for building a strong social media community and fostering meaningful connections with followers.

120. Recommend tools and resources for staying updated on social media trends and best practices.

Email Marketing

121. Create an email welcome series to onboard new subscribers and nurture them into customers.

122. Provide tips for writing effective subject lines to increase email open rates.

123. Generate ideas for compelling email newsletter content to keep subscribers engaged.

124. Recommend strategies for personalizing email campaigns to improve customer segmentation.

125. Discuss effective tactics for growing an email subscriber list organically.

126. Create a template for abandoned cart recovery emails to increase conversion rates.

127. Provide insights on A/B testing techniques for optimizing email campaign performance.

128. Generate ideas for creating enticing email exclusive offers and promotions.

129. Discuss strategies for re-engaging inactive subscribers and revitalizing email campaigns.

130. Provide tips for ensuring email deliverability and maintaining a good sender reputation.

131. Create a series of automated email workflows for lead nurturing and customer onboarding.

132. Provide tips for optimizing email deliverability and avoiding spam filters.

133. Generate ideas for personalizing email content based on subscriber preferences or behavior.

134. Discuss strategies for segmenting email lists to deliver targeted and relevant content to subscribers.

135. Create a template for conducting A/B testing on email subject lines, CTAs, or email layouts.

136. Provide insights on utilizing dynamic content in email campaigns for personalized messaging.

137. Discuss tactics for re-engaging inactive subscribers and reviving email engagement rates.

138. Generate ideas for creating compelling email newsletters that provide value to subscribers.

139. Provide tips for optimizing email templates for mobile devices and responsive email design.

140. Recommend email marketing platforms or software for efficient campaign management.

Website Optimization

141. Perform a website audit and provide recommendations for improving site speed and performance.

142. Create a template for writing persuasive call-to-action (CTA) buttons to increase conversions.

143. Provide tips for optimizing landing pages to enhance user experience and encourage action.

144. Generate ideas for creating compelling testimonials and social proof elements on website pages.

145. Discuss strategies for optimizing website navigation to improve user engagement and reduce bounce rates.

146. Provide insights on responsive design best practices for a seamless mobile browsing experience.

147. Create a template for creating an effective homepage layout that captures attention and communicates key messages.

148. Recommend strategies for improving search engine visibility and optimizing on-page SEO elements.

149. Discuss tactics for implementing conversion rate optimization (CRO) techniques to maximize website conversions.

150. Provide tips for creating a user-friendly checkout process that minimizes cart abandonment.

151. Analyze website user experience and provide recommendations for improving site navigation and usability.

152. Create a template for conducting A/B tests on website elements to optimize conversion rates.

153. Provide tips for creating persuasive product or service landing pages that drive conversions.

154. Generate ideas for adding trust signals and security badges to build credibility on the website.

155. Discuss strategies for optimizing website accessibility to cater to a wider range of users.

156. Create a template for conducting user surveys or feedback forms to gather insights on website improvements.

157. Provide insights on utilizing heatmaps and click tracking tools to analyze user behavior on the website.

158. Discuss tactics for optimizing website loading speed to enhance user experience and reduce bounce rates.

159. Generate ideas for implementing exit-intent pop-ups to capture leads or reduce cart abandonment.

160. Recommend tools or plugins for implementing live chat support on the website for real-time customer assistance.

Digital Product Creation

161. Generate ideas for creating an online course in a specific industry or skill set.

162. Provide insights on structuring and organizing digital products for optimal learning outcomes.

163. Discuss strategies for pricing and packaging digital products to maximize sales and profitability.

164. Create a template for designing visually appealing e-books or downloadable resources.

165. Provide tips for conducting market research to identify profitable digital product ideas.

166. Discuss strategies for creating high-converting sales pages for digital products.

167. Generate ideas for designing engaging video tutorials or webinars for digital product content.

168. Provide insights on creating a membership site to offer exclusive content or services.

169. Discuss tactics for promoting and launching digital products to generate buzz and attract customers.

170. Recommend tools and platforms for hosting and delivering digital products securely.

171. Discuss strategies for creating engaging and informative podcast episodes for digital content.

172. Generate ideas for creating interactive quizzes or assessments as part of digital products.

173. Provide tips for conducting market research to identify potential gaps and demand for digital products.

174. Create a template for outlining a comprehensive curriculum for an online course.

175. Discuss strategies for promoting digital products through webinars or virtual events.

176. Generate ideas for creating visually appealing infographics or data visualizations for digital content.

177. Provide insights on designing effective user interfaces for mobile apps or digital tools.

178. Discuss tactics for creating high-quality instructional videos for online courses or tutorials.

179. Create a template for developing downloadable worksheets or templates as supplementary materials.

180. Recommend tools or platforms for hosting and delivering digital products securely and efficiently.

Data Analytics and Insights

181. Generate a report on website traffic patterns and user behavior using Google Analytics data.

182. Provide insights on interpreting and analyzing key performance indicators (KPIs) for e-commerce businesses.

183. Create a template for tracking and analyzing social media engagement metrics across different platforms.

184. Discuss strategies for using customer data to personalize marketing campaigns and improve customer experiences.

185. Recommend data visualization tools and techniques for presenting business insights effectively.

186. Generate ideas for conducting surveys or feedback forms to gather valuable customer insights.

187. Provide tips for implementing marketing attribution models to assess the effectiveness of different channels.

188. Discuss strategies for leveraging customer segmentation to optimize targeting and messaging.

189. Create a template for conducting cohort analysis to understand customer retention and lifetime value.

190. Recommend tools and resources for staying updated on the latest trends and advancements in data analytics.

191. Generate insights on analyzing customer lifetime value (CLTV) and customer acquisition cost (CAC) for business growth.

192. Provide tips for utilizing cohort analysis to understand user behavior and retention patterns.

193. Create a template for conducting customer surveys or feedback forms to gather actionable insights.

194. Discuss strategies for utilizing sentiment analysis to gauge customer sentiment and brand perception.

195. Recommend tactics for tracking and measuring social media engagement metrics across different platforms.

196. Generate ideas for conducting A/B tests on website elements to optimize user experience and conversions.

197. Provide insights on using data visualization tools to present data in a visually appealing and understandable format.

198. Discuss strategies for implementing personalization techniques based on customer data and preferences.

199. Create a template for analyzing website traffic sources and conversion rates to optimize marketing efforts.

200. Recommend resources and platforms for learning data analytics skills and staying updated on industry trends.

BONUS #2: Setting Up a Passive Online Revenue Source

Ladies and gentlemen, entrepreneurs and dreamers, today we unveil a chapter that will forever alter the landscape of online business. A chapter that encapsulates the spirit of innovation and empowers individuals to forge their own paths to success. We present to you a step-by-step guide that will ignite your imagination and revolutionize the way you generate passive income in the digital realm.

Imagine a future where the digital landscape becomes your playground, where your expertise and creativity blend seamlessly with the power of GPT Chat 4 to establish a passive revenue stream that propels you towards your dreams. This is not a mere fantasy, but a tangible reality within your grasp.

In this chapter, we present a step-by-step guide that will guide you through the intricacies of setting up a passive online revenue source exclusively through GPT Chat 4. We will reveal the secrets to defining your niche, constructing an interactive chatbot, creating compelling content, promoting your offerings, monetizing your chatbot, and scaling your business to unprecedented heights.

Through each stage of this transformative journey, you will witness the remarkable synergy between human ingenuity and the boundless potential of GPT Chat 4. It is a partnership that will revolutionize the way you generate income online, giving you the tools to create a sustainable business that thrives in the digital landscape.

Step 1: Define Your Niche and Target Audience

Begin by conducting thorough market research using tools like Google Trends, SEMrush, or Buzzsumo to identify a profitable niche with sufficient demand. Define your target audience by analyzing demographics, interests, and pain points using platforms like Facebook Audience Insights or Google Analytics.

Example: If you have a passion for fitness and wellness, you might choose a niche like "home workout routines for busy professionals" targeting individuals aged 25-45 who are interested in fitness and have limited time for exercise.

Step 2: Set Up a Chatbot Using GPT Chat 4

Choose a chatbot platform that integrates with GPT Chat 4, such as Chatfuel, ManyChat, or Dialogflow. These platforms provide user-friendly interfaces for designing and deploying chatbots. Use GPT Chat 4's API to power your chatbot with natural language processing capabilities and engaging conversational abilities.

Example: Use Chatfuel to create a chatbot for your fitness niche, allowing users to interact with your workout recommendations and receive personalized fitness tips.

Step 3: Generate Compelling Content

Create high-quality content to support your chatbot and attract your target audience. Develop informative blog posts, videos, or podcasts that provide valuable insights, tutorials, and fitness tips. Optimize your content for search engines using tools like Yoast SEO or SEMrush to increase visibility and organic traffic.

Example: Produce blog posts on topics such as "Quick and Effective Home Workouts for Busy Professionals" and create video tutorials demonstrating proper exercise form and technique.

Step 4: Promote Your Chatbot and Content

Utilize various marketing channels to drive traffic to your chatbot and content. Leverage social media platforms like Instagram, Facebook, and YouTube to share engaging snippets and teasers that direct users to your chatbot. Implement email marketing campaigns using platforms like Mailchimp or ConvertKit to nurture leads and encourage chatbot engagement.

Example: Share engaging workout videos on Instagram and direct users to your chatbot for personalized workout recommendations. Offer a free downloadable e-book on "10 Essential Fitness Tips for Busy Professionals" to entice visitors to sign up for your email list.

Step 5: Monetize Your Chatbot

Implement revenue-generating strategies within your chatbot to turn it into a passive income source. Explore options like affiliate marketing, sponsored content, digital product sales, or premium subscription plans. Join reputable affiliate networks like Amazon Associates, ClickBank, or ShareASale to find relevant fitness products to promote.

Example: Partner with fitness equipment companies as an affiliate and recommend their products within your chatbot conversations. Develop premium workout plans or personalized coaching sessions available for purchase within the chatbot.

Step 6: Monitor, Analyze, and Optimize

Regularly monitor the performance of your chatbot, content, and revenue streams using analytics tools like Google Analytics or Facebook Pixel. Track metrics such as user engagement, conversion rates, and revenue generated. Analyze the data to identify trends and areas for improvement, then optimize your chatbot's responses, refine your content strategy, and enhance your monetization tactics.

Example: Use Google Analytics to track user engagement metrics such as time spent in the chatbot, click-through rates on affiliate links, and conversion rates for premium subscriptions. Identify patterns and adjust your strategies accordingly.

Step 7: Scale and Expand

As your passive revenue source gains momentum, consider scaling and expanding your offerings. Develop additional chatbots targeting different fitness niches or expand into related areas like nutrition, wellness, or mental health. Continuously innovate and adapt to meet the evolving needs of your audience.

Example: If your home workout chatbot proves successful, consider creating chatbots for nutrition guidance or meditation practices within the fitness and wellness niche.

CONCLUSION

Congratulations, trailblazers of the digital age! You have traversed the exhilarating terrain of Chat GPT-4 and delved into the extraordinary possibilities that await in the realm of online wealth generation. From building passive income streams from scratch to harnessing the power of prompts, customer support automation, content creation, and more, you have equipped yourselves with the tools to conquer the digital landscape like never before. Throughout this sensational journey, you have witnessed the transformative impact of Chat GPT-4, propelling you towards financial success with its unparalleled capabilities. You have explored real-world success stories that have shattered the norms, realizing that your dreams of financial freedom are no longer distant fantasies but tangible realities within your grasp.

By leveraging the potential of Chat GPT-4, you have gained a competitive edge, unlocking lucrative opportunities in various professions and revolutionizing the way you conduct financial analysis and investment research. You have discovered the art of crafting engaging content, optimizing your online presence, and captivating your audience with persuasive copy that drives conversions. But the revolution doesn't stop there. You have embraced the power of Chat GPT-4 in customer support and engagement, propelling your business to new heights of customer satisfaction and loyalty. You have witnessed how AI-driven insights and prompts can supercharge your productivity, creativity, and decision-making, leading you to unmatched success.

And let's not forget the remarkable bonuses that have amplified your journey to greatness. With 200 prompts to ignite your online money-making endeavors and a comprehensive guide to setting up passive online revenue sources, you have gained an arsenal of tools and knowledge that will shape your destiny.

But we don't consider this journey complete without you, the pioneers of this new era, leaving your mark. We invite you to share your honest feedback, stories of triumph, and insights gained from this extraordinary expedition. Let your voices be heard on Amazon, where your reviews will inspire and guide others on their own quests for financial independence.

Remember, you possess the power to transform your financial life and shape your own destiny. Let the sensational impact of Chat GPT-4 propel you forward, as you harness its capabilities to generate passive income, boost your online presence, and master the art of financial success. The future is here, and it is yours to seize. Embrace the potential, unleash your financial superpowers, and become the architect of your own wealth. Thank you for embarking on this extraordinary journey with us. Now, go forth and conquer the digital landscape like never before! Please consider leaving your honest feedback on Amazon and inspire others to discover the life-changing potential of Chat GPT-4. Your voice matters, and together, we will shape a future brimming with financial triumph. Unleash your financial superpowers today!

Made in the USA
Monee, IL
15 June 2023

35874322R00059